apparitions
(nines)

NAT RAHA

apparitions
(nines)

NIGHTBOAT BOOKS

NEW YORK

ISBN: 978-1-643-62239-2

Cover Art: P. Staff, *To Live a Good Life I*, 2022.
Courtesy of the artist.

Design and typesetting by Kit Schluter
Typeset in Sabon

Cataloging-in-publication data is available
from the Library of Congress

Nightboat Books
New York
www.nightboat.com

dedicated to

Sean Bonney
(1969-2019)

Nila Kamol Gupta
(1975-2021)

callie gardner
(1990-2021)

in friendship, study & courage

CONTENTS

The niner is a contemporary form of the nine-line poem, typically in sequences of nine poems. More recently, the niner consists of lines of nine syllables and/or other numerical orderings in the number of sounds or words related to the number nine.

Coined by the poet Mendoza and adopted by various innovative writers, the niner is seemingly a "sonnot," resembling a sonnet while radically departing from its conventions; a perverse sounding that adopts a masochistic containment. In this book, the nine-syllable line reads as a brash, punk, or post-punk response to the metrics of Anglophone verse. The form has allowed for experiment and study in dialect and accent, and their effect upon the language, contained in a line of nine syllables or beats.

"[…] that we share a common cause and that we are liable to the same justice, that before the world's tribunal we are held to the same responsibilities, and that in the great outline of the universal project of humankind, we are held to the same qualifications."

—AIMÉ CÉSAIRE, 1945

"It is in the process of going into the world 'beyond' that 'Europe' itself came into being. European colonial projects explain so much in the postcolonial world—how could they not explain Europe to itself?"

—PRIYAMVADA GOPAL
"On Decolonization and the University"

"As we arm ourselves with ourselves and each other, we can stand toe to toe in that rigorous loving and begin to speak the impossible—or what has always seemed like the impossible—to one another. […] if we speak the truth to each other, it will become unavoidable to ourselves."

—AUDRE LORDE
"Eye to Eye: Black Women, Hatred, and Anger"

i

[i / 1]

this of obscure cosmos /
violence,, reiterated
vivid, paused blood in fire & syn
thetics << silver & liquid
eyes stenciled brick quot
-as / authors who could not
conceive us & hold / to have live

-d im/possible gravity ,,
chilled & // all known ways

[i / 2]

decimate, un/made & horny
, our shaven flesh & locks, dined on
black beans, corn & sugar, vagabonds,
tinkers, tricksters & jailbirds <
had demanded our bodies O
fascist rags, codes & division
s systematic flesh & capitals

nostalgia imposed & gen
der/ivative nations ,, soil *f≈*

[i / 3]

agree: your logic treacherous
political & philosophic
„ distribution of thought & activ
-ity engineer'd [#] divest
meant hot policing & exot
-ic / *but some of us want to keep*

our jobs" in yur demand that we flesh
nice for being & pills / had
abolished yur entitlements,, our

[i / 4]

sexes & flesh constituted
from the women & femmes who charged

you: pale & sweating majorities
/ smears & intonations
assured arrogant thieves /$
if your violence a source of pleasure
/ we trust our anxious days & juts
where once bridges, borders,,

decline winter bones;; gorgeous, warm

[i / 5]

grrrl // if we are citizens
of nowhere, a threat to the tone &
image;; composed / lace cute
we divine femmes no here to disse
-ct your impositions >>
so late in the day, bark organs
in casual violence: your pleasure
excruciate living / &
the beauty about our eyelines

[i / 6]

this decades-old violence, for board
stars & black salt, she said the possi-
ble diminished / order admini
stirred names, ~~ff norm~~

haar & solstice eyed / fall into
the waged day , turbulent shimmer
out of discourse traded close, pinned
/ ordinary trappings & verse
to squat ,, dis / locate

[i / 7]

in nationhood, your reveries
five hundred truncated years, we
dined on stolen whisky, tar, minis
-terial bones / forced to find work
a rustic allegory, regen
narrating cities & ag/gressions
light & nature false con
dition'd : cohered by skins our
/ separated, crashed ⸢, lit⸥

[i / 8]

at trial : yur crimes of invention
in my charred gold minidress /
cremated homes, debt && circuits
capital commission & hate

dined on flour, divine salt &&
threads of your flags ,, aroused,
our vulgar comedy, drives &
erotics, silenced >/ your beliefs
& rituals :: disintegrating,

[i / 9]

[≈] we impossible siblings,, lobes
sore, close hairs & gleaming / our
traumas dismissed / bitter salt stream
-ing cheeks, spark / structurally

yur lavish/ious divisions
, devaluations, institut
-ions, blood,, harmonics
/ of work, migration & con
jugal / flicker, track memory

ejected from the cities of live
-s possible aperture & tone
/ eyes & text flow depriv-
[[pacify / structure—

                    puzzles && crapchat ortho
                    dox / visions & wretching
                ,, focus out of drift w/
                                varnish
            , done gold, put
                        your warmth by the
            skin of the next grrrl
                            , air drops off

[i i / 2]

tongues, no snow archaic gener
-ate/ors & markets strung
illuminated from fears
:: hold your posture / eyes grow alive
against the constitution of continents

/ we dream to raze what forged
our agoraphobia ,, looks over
lowlands / isle-shriek, reach your form
-er silence f. — —.

[i i / 3]

we, the invisible: streets strewn
w/ feathers, our solitude
—negative reveries vibrant
squatting schools & rulings, yur
nights ripped by fire, disinvest
-ed / the deepened particular
of fleshes, our / memory embodied
, itching, wet on the union jack
your truths will be rerooted—

[i i / 4]

all riches, all fruits, all cotton

that was worked ⧸;   the narrow
administration yur   cash flow
worlds, pleas/ures   force his
they'd deem not work   stories under de-

               privation ((downward bracket, closed
               ripped the crux of our instruments
               / rot bodies,, driving urgent
               project, protest, lunar ec—

≪ lips/is , in the devi
ance, for longing, turning
across flesh / our love ≠
directions in the worlding

      cobbled archives / secure
      deleted myths & revolts
      mimeos dissolved & in
      heritance , wages —]
                  slay their
      the/atres :   impossible . now .

[i i / 6]

bred through dutiful, us, assimi
-lar, metropole a[n] ~~re~~/order
remain awake, sign transient
you/r bare hands & freezing
        wrecks talents : glam/our
        flakes, grrrl forget the legible
        inclusive && diminished
        eating twice a day, ⊣ fucking
        against the national interest

[i i / 7]

-tion / fuchsia & scarlet flight
/ under threat of eliminat
[nine beats placed / here]
living on the edge of the city
amplifies literate skin /

        —on the tongue / devasting
        particular[s,,] reforged in
        an everyday violence, which you
        call the work of history /

since the soul in our poetic—
falls onto / echoed fabric
composite creolite britain is
orchestrations / cultural
breath divested// dips glottals

that they believe in their whiteness
viral fictions & departments
monodrama / & image
, interiors , customs & screens

[i i / 9]

sung the winter, caustic, unabett
-ed black eyes & woolmark [#] sing

                    how it weighs to hold against
                    the basic synthesis of your day

          [ill.] tides we creat
/ures, queens & vaults, lines
& ⤳ / neglected, light fades
cranes, rustic metropolitan
sense—allegories deceased

iii

[i i i / i]

for Jacqueline Frost

such that we are fucked, *toget-*
//her, fighting for our love
our aesthetic array split
-s sides on vinyl / gives the

> > > > > *queers a need to blues*, in wings
> > > > > their eyes stop-start a cabaret
> > > > > that doesn't come to dance , strewn
> > > > > in dreaming, hunger / known &
> > > > > synthetic, melodies rupt.

[i i i / 2]

of the possible *is their droplet*
eyes, climatic quits to feed
sheer shoulders polyester—

carries the damage into truth
& pinning
echoes on a snare
saline in vox & lyric ;

our circuits fragile ,, *thread the*
spangle permanent rose, writing
opaque
undoes our own straps——

[i i i / 3]

                              -ble, royal & north estates /
                        of continents / dream to raze
                              abstract markets & vendors

        headstroke , ex
                        / hale &
turbines
            behind the ear /
        gaze old & beats to
                        dan
                              ce by
            ⫻grow eyes in night we
                              keep
            alive 'gainst the construction
                        incentivized hunger, falli

[i i i / 4]

// stole metrics from fags
or molluscs / an endless
artifice, synthesis,, viol/

    ate, trill w/rapt what hoard
      dried, stripped & itching /
        speaks surrealizations

disposed : britain, crying, filthy
e/laborate error , waiting
,, drops for the heat of the color

[i i i / 5]

after Anne Boyer

having discarded the formula
ry, salvaging sake of fates, tal
-k back to fascists sure [#]
we were advising blockades, noi
-se, desire, orgasms &
solidarities unseen on this

        burning continent, we: pyres,
        shields, new tides, your breach
        'd reacting town. elated.

[i i i / 6]

with lines from Frank O'Hara's "Homosexuality"

/ *& down the lengthening shadow*
divine ones / fuse streets
with the forms of beauty to be

in the creopole /
                    dragged up
centuries / lust-seared
wilding the nature of light

            switched-out / served abjection
                    squatted for heat & harmonics
        , weight borne against her body /

[i i i / 7]

detached formulaic
our
    saturate eyes
        chroma
-tic , brittle , split, flaked w/out

      queer composite undergird
        -s sequined in our blesséd

eva/ po
therwise   r   dazed from newest spectacle
    ,,   a   left screeching in tonal threads—
  de   t e s in being o
   pen
     dent to depth

[i i i / 8]

          delve out of prescriptions, vacuum

split—

    polyphonic

, lips resolute

    activated

synthetic / musing bodies

    re/versing the monoculture

      ,,

    its clocks belie us in easy

    fiction; emergent, dizzying—

dusk shards hanging our

      animate lives of the present

these basic rooms / of lives,
sycamore drip / the throats
of us,, grip vines , ceiling
tend/rills_[.]   forgets her
meds—
    scope focal & thins
rout/ines these spines from
such breath
     falls

          ,,
        dis   -se
       growth these twenty-five, the
          sol   '9s
           ve   de
            fabri
          ca
        te   —

[i v / ɪ]

at these peaks in yur histor
-y of reactions̶,̶ skull pulse
in such total hostility
claw cult/ure[s]: bleached,

amnesiac, a false im-
aginary, fragile tide in
-cendary ǂ slice ceaseless
ads, newsprint & telegrams
: pockmarked , revol/ve

[i v / 2]

in excess of yur laws &
dichotomies ⫽ circular spar
-k turned forward, detuned
hunger shrunk on the waged/

flesh rooted in these we
salt water / satin decimal
live fever split ⸴/ been
thieving do[l]e eyed, harrow
flaunt & litter centuries, yur

[i v / 3]

abandoned on love, we queers
left to own our ⌊⌊* she
/lls decades sore, nos
-talgia out, diminished, vib
-brate into & out of taut

       bare unequal dist., thres
       /held skin in likeness, your
       memories split & wired,
       dejected, weight frays &

[i v / 4]

they that would revoke this flesh
in fear of fictions breathed
what is given the flow, structure
to materialize, w/ love
& capital, in life #

that your image speaks so sparse /
coarse & hollow cognitions
, overdetermined, exchange
-value, brand, appropriate＝

[i v / 5]

as all the exits shut reverse
the town hall each riot van
engine removed // chassis
neomarine ecology
sensate vessels history
bitter buried sands, ride it up
the walk, seem before tarmac

babe hold. frequencies
to be removed from the air

[i v / 6]

more: dependent cages unwrit
ten / stretch verbs revised
, bonded—victors, capital, etc.
fly no fl/ags as evaporate
currency, stone, know this hand,

yur devious logics, neo-
occupation of words, senti
ment bare grammar of bodies
tangential, trained, maneuvered

what spells, war, yur desper/ate
internal coloniality
riots, food , 38 harvest
-s arctic & lungs on fire
/ relations between things
, exchanged, labor, wages, dis–

possessions, the centuries we
disinte/grate, found new feeling
-s ,, consciousness, actions /

[i v / 8]

rat scour / breach circuits
/ dynamite what walls you dream
opulence & appropria
-tions, statues, cloud cover;
con/demned to reside in
swirling floods, fauna, of rubble
& order, deforestation
-s, toxicities / assem-
bled you. e/vaporate—

what futures you seize & split
chaos & falsehoods, yur pla
-gue of affections, yur extra-
legal arm //

       our specter:
the reparation of centuries,
yur thieved & horded borders
dissolve formations &
patriots / block bodies

'gainst yur empyre / raids.

V

[v / i]

werk this filth . decimate
spring buds teeter // gaze
lines what want shoulders &

                              our acrylic, dubious
                              angelic / spines' depth ≠
                                   [   ]

                    [   ]
          [   ]

, mouths across cherry crush

[v / 2]

in the hyperreal of this beau-
ty, this wear, fashion-bodily
, dyke bitch being smeared color sync

—such potential faggotry,, the
-se shades pressed to you

[o]'re gorgeous pre/tend
change of use anthropos
in your blesséd vulnerabil
-ity ,/ remember what we live

[v / 3]

aharmonic swells through the
spatial , torso & limbs , their /
con/text split off flesh_bring
your needed self around its branching

        // what is humbled merely
        future source f/or meaning
        like vacuum dreaming, like
        alternate spectra of visible

        dizzy gold flaked on sheets ,

[v / 4]

twitching in the dream
our / gazettes, archives,
den rose hip flesh delicate
fledge creopolitan //

sleeve stitched fragility bare
what waking calls skin , tended, strapped
,, feminized, assembled, type
our scattered belonging

-written, isolated, disappear-

[v / 5]

after Alberta Whittle, between a whisper and a cry *(2019)*

invitation to reverie, po-
        ssible skins~~
               connect
                    lilts & flows into psyche , they

enter the frame , the gallery
    known bitter to lash & languidi
        -ty in prospect / your camera

eyes hem toward your flesh
        centered / rising in halls
               yet the storms continue to come

[v / 6]

after Kindness, Something Like A War *(2019)*

in softness, as weapon , casting
        logics callous from us ,
arms as air, as sea , sensation
                    spun , unbinds in refusal,, slow
                        sequence of days expanse

                    retuned / keep near your
                            pastel / tone's depth sights a
                    heart on keys you grant yourself
                            femme vox affections unfurl

[v / 7]

course edges ecstatic

                dissolved w/ love , open soul
      all eyes generosity

          we gossip as daggers as tender
as chiffon , we feed as commune

sneak laughter , lust across

    borders , hirsterical
        / our insolent freedom
           armed w/ rigorous loving

[v / 8]

                              between scarcity , our disper
                              sals holding eyes lines wants
                              years known, accumulated—

        tracing flesh on flesh , candescent
        / gathered wrists in lyric—
                        lay queer delica/cies
                        cour/sing // reassembling—

                        to face, adjunct, your season,
                        of solitudinous days

[v / 9]

                              sure, of these days all fact will be
          thrown scold nebulae between the
livid & liminal , compress
                    sketch & sculpt yur tendons, /
              , what gives energetics to these

                              in the writhing accumulate /
                              populate asset & fictions

              unmaking the scope of labels
          lines wayward soar on no keys

vi

[v i / ɪ]

we creopolitan : our
c/hanging & relations ,
our senses of bodying
,, whispers, humming to know flesh
sensate taste salt weather cane
/ humidity woven through /
dis/placed, to be anyw-
here, all possible futures
undo logics of land/ed

[v i / 2]

spirit of blood, fibers , swell
, marxisms , estuaries,
trans/lations, stolen lit
-eratures—
                    all we have survive
-d / frequencies embedded
in the body ⊬ cracked open
y/our streets constituted
:: autonomy , gentrification,
citadels, stories, resist—

[v i / 3]

lockdown, vacuum, famine, derelic
-tion, sanctions, engineered
, cleared, the hands / mouth,
prospect living rui/nation
in yur ruling domicile , in

moonrise pulls us out into
days, bares gravity at tide

-fernos & housing washout, lie
comms junk / hunger sprawl

[v i / 4]

digitals thread our dispersed
con/text of containment, de-

                    tuned, diverted , flesh parched—

            on the prospects of plague lips
                    gaze & words thirst, aligning
                a communal current, dripping

walled, undaze:: sub/mergent
                            into senses, swelling as we
                try$_{[,]}$ hold air out toward each other

[v i / 5]

                        glassed eyes, petty urban re-
                        fractures, asphalt && cobble
                        over accumulate roofing,
                        liquefied, our days optics
        warp thirsting algorhythmic
engorge
          , held by echo
      ringing,
            visible horrors

             , dissolve synthetic pleasant
                streets speak plague hirstory

[v i / 6]

schema di/vesting black & brown
breath burnt ab/andonded
nest synthetic pale on pray
screech bitter salvation prized

light disdain calls benevolent
neoliberal tears cellular
carbon based / carbon torn
stones & plaster time contained to fail

continues its ordinary

[v i / 7]

systematic denigrate breath, char
coal golden sick on quotidian
/ contiguous memories of yur
violence embedded ,—smoke
screened / accumulation on
crisis horror, iridescent thrown
earthen cuts to claim, to clear

, flow flag blood, pure[,] decay
removes how the earth is walked

[v i / 8]

this: their war, absolute silence
, no molecules / vibrate /
vacuum immiseration

    hands, fuck all most days, social
    smeared newsprint zeros no touch
    hungering for scent, variation
    ,, plague dredge, yet the rich seem

    to have forgotten how to die /

    beneath cobble, cramped bones

[v i / 9]

memories proscribed & the theft of
season / spread on capital, com
-modity pleas/ed daze dregs
in the social hierarchy, our
deletion se/cure, blinkered
police orbital , t(e)ased &
powered, reduced 100 years
your next blossom & fire, no
outlier body which to speak

vii

[v i i / 1]

of all taken from bodies
our remaining hunger /, &
w/ it yur pricetags on sustenance

, delayed payments, imaginary
chains of power, purchase /
what we call to abolish¬

we re/assembled our
affections & solidarities
our cracked, efflorescent hands,

[v i i / 2]

in their abandonment our black &
brown s/kin , respiri//
rations / partic(ular dry

        be/longing to unstitch border
        -s practicing quiet to gather

        coloniality's pile-up

collectives for mourning (re)emerge

    ears out to wire poetic
    against total policing

[v i i / 3]

on the stand, list yur horrors
, proclamations & divestments
pour blood from the crown & ideo.
, your archaic, printed murders
bludgeon, civilize to this day

'gainst the name of yur inflictions
yur rubble & basic hatred

turn hands to/gather, / /
stolen our lives & bodies back

[v i i / 4]

                sure, w/ yyr meager hoarded fragment

of earth, gold store your germs
/ & spoils, defended

from the right to roam, the decayed,
& undead. we declare centu

                -ries buckled in vio/lent
                , torn & shredded viral logic
                its impossible defense

                hands shatter the perimeter

[v i i / 5]

                    of actions fluid : our hir
        -stories / all you have accu
                    mulated, coercive system

-s of the separable—ur sick
closed sensations & borders

                         in the trauma of movement, sed
                            -imented thru layers of spirit
            „ what fledgling you force from land
            whims of em/pyre, decline

[v i i / 6]

& each extra minute in/
habiting toxicity, sure,
capital's youth poisoned
denigrate oxygen & partic
-ulates, the logic of what years
have been stolen from us, our
faster conservative deaths ,,/
decayed, barren & suckered
tattered palms, sanitized

[v i i / 7]

& frays lines scarce to our
bodies, psyches & nutrition
years shadowed ocular /
know this harshest winter forecast

isolate our derelict arms
decant glamor, scent, oiled
medicinal, tending, ankled soft
in grievous color, gather
—wedge
precious cycles of repetition

so how about that flaming global
order,, contagion of our re-
volting looks / mouths & passion
-s, yur horror that we could bloom
scripting lashes in digital /

from yur genes, impure, b/light
collectivize a means to body
urgency scored to futures,

revoking yur vocabulary

[v i i / 9]

in the attempt to establish
norms,, old guard *keep the country*
moving w/ contagion, herds, ex-
cess & slaughter / new flood plains
we dole hounds, surface ruptures

reorient senses, skills
[#] radical imaginary
belief in chaotic possible
we live in fabricating this

[v i i i / 1]

after José Esteban Muñoz's The Sense of Brown *(2013)*

~~dis~~/organization, harsh,

       indig/nation of houses
       our trappings & dis/placement
       , vacancies, movements , crossing
belts & bridges ,, intensive
hope, unit care emergent crys
-talline under skin & soul

task to touch the space of sensa
-tion , dynamic , dynamite

[v i i i / 2]

left little of what nutrition
hazel kernel cocoa dusk write
                    relation / reveal hands
               in depths pleasure brown somatic

               thawed out, turn up soil , enspirit
                    accrued ancestral , known, re-

woke in the days longest
say it— *feel music in your eye*
-s, *rain-*   & the hardest truths

[v i i i / 3]

necks eased auburn / in
the woods

                          bares the grief /

loss we leave our friends by
future groove longing in queer

            , your located california
            fingers —

                                          s —

            s — s

            a single trace of study :
            aged oak surrounded by
            apartments we used to live

[v i i i / 4]

& grrrl, who're you to abandon
the beautiful // jettison

       ways of being, pursed on edge
       on song, speed , surf/ace

       divine, tuned , luxurious:
       the earliest known sensations
       adorned / silk woven /
       learning your rhythm from canvas
       / lubrication for your soul

[v i i i / 5]

inaugurate our futures—

in your face of the wrecking
of our lives, suffocation

, naïve liberal admissions
given yur occupation of land

-s, our thoughts & centuries
stolen hands & appendages

dye cut water & oxygen ⦸
axing the health in the nation

[v i i i / 6]

o tragic national consensus
tearing continental floes /

classify, evidence, carbon
        date, pulled up medieval bones

        & all enspirited life
we will exorcise your explo
        rations from all land, ocean
, all yr orders & abstractions—

the disappeared will live

[v i i i / 7]

justice is a practice to
unfold, re:verse the future

turn the truth up from soil /
in the everyday / compelled
all that crashes w/ pandemic
all that's held against need

& after our affections
dozed regressive histories
//, bloom alternate truths

[v i i i / 8]

in sparse winters our death
apartments crushed besides
bare we now all is our breathing

friend, what is left for us
dance effluvial prospects
friend, walk the flood toward

beacons, lunar ascendant
decomposers overrun the
remainder of verberate streets

[v i i i / 9]

before the world's tribunal ::
& if the crisis in your method
-s of inhabiting the earth
diminish futures' scope
our refusal of your ways
, orientations of hours
& days, bodyminds & souls
all empires have known how
to save are their heads

ix

[i x / 1]

        decolonization: the demo
  -lition of what you have stood for
                . all power to survivors, all
    power to the executed,
                    deported & murdered /
we, the ancestry, exiled
         in the upset of your orders
     hills tracts, circular jail
          stolen subterranean joy /

[i x / 2]

in the demolition of your mon
-uments,, emit alternate light
we live counter to exclusions
, extractions, accumulations
violent reorders of earth

logics of possession, exploit
slave & deteriorate imperial
pull labor w/ force from life

revoke capital's stage

[i x / 3]

given we outlived your senten
-ces of death, life & deportation
given your sentiment to exile,

undermining status, hirstory
every truth another match
each lived future dynamite

our laughter, beats audacious
blown culture, police lines
unsounding british gravity

[i x / 4]

wretched atmospheric / fear
volatile mirrors & hatred
your storms of occupation
hillsides, water & temples
dividing heat, bodies & minds

the food from our real mouths
, commodities / millions
set spells to eviscerate /
weapons & abstractions /

[i x / 5]

now in yur ruptured history
, crystalline crushed worldview /
dissolve etchings, erosion
your voyages & gunboats
remembering , rememory

    our

      traumas in the street
     a negative public fleshed
     of compressed cycles solar
     groundswell, rhythm[s], ̶l̶l̶l̶l̶ ̶l̶l̶l̶l̶ ̶l̶l̶l̶l̶

[i x / 6]

in our forms of appearance
here to end this eternity
constellations & cyclones
these earthly suffocations
architectures, mutations
orbit of vessels & capital
asserted shards & flames
all we became in the provocat
-tions, particles, alarmed

[i x / 7]

                              membranes deteriorate
toxicity—our fevers
              & constellations , trying to

     unstick garish riches
          preached to scold all corners
     patterns for thought, feeling, action

                    & hold blessings ,, pleasures,
          oxygen , &if fear tears
               look me in the eyes w/ love

[i x / 8]

& yet, future not in waiting
/ tearing roofs off weapons
factories, calling in rain
, spell against occupations

                        drive
                            a wedge in economics
                        of maiming, borders, displacement
                        bitter centuries we've survived

                orbits germinate, deject
                empyre's swollen gravity

[i x / 9]

                      implicate substance untapped
                 restart today's ethics
                        while our heads, hands /
targeted words remain / ob
-solesce orders : criminal
   [& pathological , bodymind
                   -s live defiant, frayed
              , , felt & strained mutuality
         chaotic gulfs of multitude

apparitions was written during a period experienced as temporal reversal, rupture and compression, 2017-2021. On June 14th, 2017, seventy-two people—the majority of who were Black and brown—were killed in the fire at Grenfell Tower, a twenty-four-story apartment block in West London. For many of us engaged in housing struggles, and in the radical history of London and the UK from anti-racist and anti-colonial perspectives, Grenfell was the amalgam of everything we knew regarding the "organized abandonment" and neglect that comes with private property oriented towards maximizing profits and a state that considers poor Black and brown people, especially Muslims, to be disposable. Grenfell echoed the history of the New Cross Fire in South East London, in which thirteen Black teenagers were killed, in January 1981. Believed to have been started by fascists during a period of numerous arson attacks on Black and Asian community spaces in London, the New Cross Fire was met with silence and inaction from the state and the media. Both events led to mass political mobilizations, led by Black and Asian communities, in the city. In the midst of the ethno-nationalist political backlashes of Brexit, Trump, Bolsonaro, Orbán, and Modi, among others, Grenfell felt like a moment where time stopped. The backlash reversing the clock: revoking the promises of "progress" and "equality" made by neoliberal capitalist multiculturalism, while actively suppressing and criminalizing dissent and marginalized people.

The first section of apparitions was penned in December 2017 in response to an attack by the British right wing media on Action for Trans Health, an autonomous trans healthcare organization. We were targeted for our mutual aid practices and our abolitionist politics. I'd co-founded the Edinburgh chapter of the organization at the start of that year—we co-authored a widely circulated "Trans Health Manifesto" which was quoted in these attacks. This attack was one of many that targeted leftist organizations, groups, intellectuals, activists and academics—especially on Black and brown womxn, trans, non-binary, and gender non-conforming people, and trans and non-binary people more broadly. These attacks targeted us on the grounds of our anti-colonial, anti-racist, anti-Zionist, pro-trans and queer work across political and social organizing, and cultural and intellectual production. Watching friends, comrades, and colleagues respond to such attacks, I witnessed responses that practiced solidarity; countering reactionary arguments with truth, intelligence and wit, and occasionally legal counsel, while making space for recovery and recuperation in the aftermath of the attacks.

In November 2019, we learned of the death of our friend, the poet Sean Bonney. Sean has been a major influence for many writers and leftists in the UK, Europe, and USA. He demonstrated political impetus and possibilities in poetry and poetics, and in doing so, underlined the role of poetry in critique, action, and the radical imagination. Sean's book *The Commons* (2011) had a major influence on my writing and politicization in particular—

I had returned to it, and to recordings of Sean reading from it, at the outset of writing *apparitions*. The shock and grief of Sean's loss were compounded by the political disintegration of the 2019 UK General Election, which saw the Tories defeating the socialist program of Jeremy Corbyn, and the onset of the COVID-19 pandemic in early 2020. We witnessed the rapid decline and rupture of the capitalist economy and its social fabric amid a rampantly racist and xenophobic "Hostile Environment" legislated by the state. In the face of slow responses by the state—followed by excessive policing and mass death—the pandemic was met with strategies of mutual aid and support, strategies that had made our lives possible for many years prior.

Following the murder of George Floyd by police in Minneapolis, Minnesota in summer 2020, Black Lives Matter reiterated that breath is a political condition, that anti-Black state violence needs to be stopped, and that the police are best abolished. During these times, many of us were reminded that we've witnessed the collapse of empires before, while those in charge cling to their last vestiges of wealth, resources, and social engineering; that the vacuum is engineered, socially, politically, economically, culturally and historically; that through collective action in the everyday, we can redistribute the possibility of life in and against racist states.

At the time of writing in Summer 2022, the public inquiry into Grenfell has yet to lead to any charges or substantive justice. The public inquiry into the Coronavirus pandemic in the UK seems unlikely to bring substantive justice either—not to those individuals affected by the deaths of frontline workers, nor does it seem likely that it will instigate any serious social redress for the hardship and grief caused by the UK government's response to the pandemic and its economic fallout (the latter spiraling further downwards by Russia's imperialist war against the Ukraine). Structural and institutional racisms remain pervasive, even as they are officially denied by the state.

The work and struggles of radical Black, Indigenous, and brown movements and people across the last four to five decades have shown us that justice rarely comes from the state—given that the same states are still to reconcile and understand their hi[r]storical crimes of settler-colonialism and dispossession, the exploitation of life, labor and land through slavery, indenture, extractivism, ecocide, and genocide. A perennial question of how we practice justice in the face of this remains—for which there are many practices, many answers.

The poetics of the last one hundred plus years has demonstrated poetry's power as a direct mode of communication that can cut through times of diatribes and violence. The niner is a form attuned to speed and constraint. They are brief containers to feel through, polemicize, and remember—to communicate the stakes of the everyday harassment and structural violence that are the lives of ourselves, our friends and our loves. For possibility, contra disposability. They shed light on the glitter and heat of our creopolitian, queer, and trans lives, in and through their collective formations.

ACKNOWLEDGMENTS

These poems were written in solidarity during times of crisis and grief, weathered through friendship, study, poetics, collectivity, care, music, dancing, art, and love. The poems have been shaped by conversations and dialogues with friends and collaborators, enriched by the generosity of ideas and spirit. Extending my deepest thanks to Mijke van der Drift, Jackqueline Frost, Salomé Honório, Mendoza, Nisha Ramayya, Jackie Wang, Adam Bainbridge, Grietje Baars, Sequoia Barnes, Jay Bernard, Anne Boyer, Anni Cameron, Anthony Capildeo, Gloria Dawson, Nish Doshi, Tanya Floaker, Razan Ghazzawi, Harry Josephine Giles, Sarah Golightley, Laura Guy, Luca Hedlund, Raisa Kabir, Tarek Lakhrissi, Peter Manson, Gemma Moncrieff, Shamira Meghani, Lola Olufemi, Claricia Parinussa, Raju Rage, Azad Ashim Sharma, Kuchenga Shenjé, Samuel Solomon, and Alberta Whittle.

Versions of these poems have previously appeared in the following publications: *We Want It All: An Anthology of Radical Trans Poetics* (Andrea Abi-Karam & Kay Gabriel (eds), Nightboat Books, 2020); *Makar/Unmakar: Twelve Poets in Scotland* (Calum Rodger (Ed.), Tapsalteerie, 2019); *Rehearsing Hospitalities 3* (Frame Contemporary Art Finland, 2021); *SEEING* (Sounds Now, 2022); and in the magazines *&SHY*, *Arc Poetry Magazine*,

Artichoke (English/German), *At Practice*, *CKZ Journal* (English/Czech), *Counterflows at Home zine*, *Datableed*, *Gutter*, *Ill Pips: The Poets' Hardship Fund*, *Kohl Journal*, *Senna Hoy* (English/French). Thank you to the editors and the translators behind these publications.

Versions of these poems appeared in a zine issued by Socio Distro (Leith, Scotland, 2019), produced as nine permutations across eighty-one copies—each with a unique ordering of twenty-seven poems taken from across the first five sections of the sequence. These publications were produced for the occasions of *Resisting Relations* (Goldsmith College, London, June 2019) and *Arika Episode 10: A Means Without End* (Glasgow, November 2019).

My deepest thank you to Gia Gonzales for your editorial insights, to Stephen Motika, Lindsey Boldt, and the rest of the team at Nightboat for supporting this work.

Dr. Nat Raha is a poet and activist-scholar whose previous books of poetry include of *sirens, body & faultlines* (2018), *countersonnets* (2013), and *Octet* (2010). Her work has appeared in *100 Queer Poems* (2022), *We Want It All: An Anthology of Radical Trans Poetics* (2020), *Liberating the Canon: An Anthology of Innovative Literature* (2018), on *Poem-a-Day*, and in *South Atlantic Quarterly*, *TSQ: Transgender Studies Quarterly*, *Transgender Marxism*, and *Wasafiri Magazine*. With Mijke Van der Drift, she co-edits the *Radical Transfeminism* zine and has co authored articles for *Social Text*, *The New Feminist Literary Studies* (2020), and the book *Trans Femme Futures: Abolitionist Ethics for Transfeminist Worlds* (2024). Nat completed her PhD in queer Marxism at the University of Sussex, and is Lecturer in Fine Art Critical Studies at the Glasgow School of Art.

NIGHTBOAT BOOKS

Nightboat Books, a nonprofit organization, seeks to develop audiences for writers whose work resists convention and transcends boundaries. We publish books rich with poignancy, intelligence, and risk. Please visit nightboat.org to learn about our titles and how you can support our future publications.

The following individuals have supported the publication of this book. We thank them for their generosity and commitment to the mission of Nightboat Books:

Kazim Ali, Anonymous (5), Ava Avnisan, Jean C. Ballantyne, Bill Bruns, V. Shannon Clyne, The Estate of Ulla Dydo, Photios Giovanis, Amanda Greenberger, David Groff, Parag Rajendra Khandhar, Vandana Khanna, Shari Leinwand, Johanna Li, Elizabeth Madans, Martha Melvoin, Care Motika, Elizabeth Motika, The Leslie Scalapino – O Books Fund, Amy Scholder, Thomas Shardlow, Ira Silverberg, Benjamin Taylor, Jerrie Whitfield and Richard Motika, and Issam Zineh

This book is made possible, in part, by grants from the New York City Department of Cultural Affairs in partnership with the City Council and the New York State Council on the Arts Literature Program.

INDEX OF FIRST LINES